FAST CASH

How to Make a Great Second Income by Selling Used Items from Garage Sales, Yard Sales, Thrift Shops, and Flea Markets

ERIC MICHAEL

Fast Cash: Flipping Used Items

How to Make a Great Second Income by Selling Used Items from Garage Sales, Yard Sales, Thrift Shops, and Flea Markets

By

Eric Michael

Table of Contents

PREFACE

Are you looking for a unique and fun way to make some extra money doing what you like to do?

Would you like to start your own home business or second income selling items that you can often find for pocket change, or even for free?

If you answered '**Yes**' to either of these questions, then the *Fast Cash* system is for you. The beauty of the Fast Cash system is its flexibility. Anybody can make significant money using this system, regardless of their background knowledge, location, and computer skills. Readers are given multiple selling options that have been proven money makers, and the opportunity to select the direction that appeals to them.

Why do 90% of readers of home business opportunity books fail to take action and launch successful income streams? #1, many of these books are dry and do not "engage" the reader, and #2 they do not motivate readers sufficiently. Many of these books fail because the author does not identify with their readers.

Fast Cash, on the other hand, is written explicitly with the reader's best interests in mind. The material is straightforward and easy to apply. The principles delivered in the book were developed directly from practices that have worked well for over twelve years, and the background research behind the principles is specified. Readers are also given direction on many sources to develop their own research abilities, so that they can enhance their background knowledge and even add new income sources to those learned here in *Fast Cash*.

If you have read our first book *Almost Free Money*, you are already familiar with methods of information delivery in this series. Readers are provided a lot of content in a very concise manner, and many areas are enhanced with real experiences of the author in regard to the flipping of used items for profit.

Here are two recent reader reviews from *Almost Free Money*:

"This book contains very detailed information and excellent ideas for people who would like to earn money through collecting and recycling scrap materials. The author also covers a bit about reselling clothing, collectibles, and other items, but the real wealth here is in learning how to recycle scrap for cash. There are even useful links provided at the end of the book for those who want to find out more, and the author also has blog and Facebook sites. Well-written, easy to understand, and full of great information!"

"I like the fact that the author talks about his own experience and gives details on how he started his business and expanded it. The book is very well structured, easy to read, enjoyable and motivating. It's a great guide that explains all the steps you need to take in order to find items that people would usually throw away, and sell them on eBay or Amazon. The author also gives a huge list of items that can bring a generous income, but the best thing is that it teaches the readers how to find their own items and become experts at spotting something that would bring them money."

The same style is applied to *Fast Cash*. Whether you are just beginning your flipping business or you have been selling used items for years, you will learn valuable tips and tricks that are found in no other books outside the Almost Free Money series. Welcome aboard and join us in this cool and profitable adventure that is the Fast Cash system.

ABOUT THE AUTHOR

Eric Michael is married and is a proud father of two young boys. He enjoys family outings and many outdoor activities, including garage sale shopping, fishing, hunting and camping.

The information provided in the *Fast Cash* and the Almost Free Money series was compiled after twelve years of internet research and personal experiences developed a unique skill set – the ability to find a diverse selection of very low priced items that could be sold on the internet for surprisingly good money.

In those twelve years, Mr. Michael has sold well over 10,000 unique items on the internet, most of which were located for under $1. Those 10,000+ items averaged over 500% profit over the buy price of each item. The *Fast Cash* and *Almost Free Money* systems have given his family a significant second income. This second income has allowed his family to go on some memorable vacations, and eliminated the necessity for child care.

Many products that are comparable to *Fast Cash* and *Almost Free Money* are offered by "internet gurus" for $25-100 on the internet, which price the product out of the reach of the people who need the product most. *Almost Free Money* has received better reader reviews than almost all of them. *Fast Cash* expands on the ideas offered in *Almost Free Money*, delves into many nuances of selling used items, and adds several vital income stream niches to readers' portfolios.

Mr. Michael has gone on to develop a popular website titled Garage Sale Academy that incorporates portions of Almost Free Money, and expands into other arenas of profiting from flipping garage sale, thrift store and flea market finds, as well as helping garage sale hosts make maximum cash at their own sales. He also hosts Facebook fan pages for Almost Free Money and Garage Sale Academy, as well as a Garage Sale Blog and Forum.

He has also written books titled Garage Sale Superstar: How to Make the Most Money Possible at your Garage Sale, Yard Sale, Rummage Sale, Estate Sale, or Tag Sale and Garage Sale Safety: How to Make Your Garage Sale Safe and Avoid Garage Sale Scams, and recently released the softcover book and DVD versions of Almost Free Money.

FAST CASH: A START-UP GUIDE

Getting started flipping is very easy and cheap. But, it is important that you accomplish several things BEFORE you start buying used items to sell:

1. Find your **picking niche**: Where do you like to shop for used items? Locating inventory should be fun! Do you like yard sale picking? Do you shop a lot at second-hand stores like <u>Goodwill and Salvation Army</u>? Perhaps you like to find free items and fix them up, part out collectible items, or sell scrap metal.

2. Find an **inventory niche**: What types of items are you interested in? Figure out if you want to specialize in one particular area like collectibles, used media items, used clothing, outdoor items, kids clothes and toys, etc. It's easiest to sell in a category that you already have background knowledge in. You may also choose to buy in a variety of categories. That's how I started flipping garage sale finds, but we will get more into that later.

3. **Storage**: The room that you have for storage may determine your inventory purchasing. If you have plenty of room for storing bulky items, you can sell whatever you want. If you are confined to a small closet or set of shelves because you live in an apartment or dorm room, you will have to sell small items that you can sell quickly. If at all possible, work on finding yourself a roomy storage area, so that you can add

bookshelves to store media items like books, DVDs, CDs, and eBay inventory.

4. **RESEARCH**: Garage sale research is where you can really get a leg up on your competition, and it is covered in-depth in *Almost Free Money*. Start looking at completed eBay listings and Amazon pages to figure out what to look for that you can make good, fast money.

5. Budgeting and Accounting: Figure out **how much money you have to spend on inventory** each week. Make yourself a spreadsheet on Excel, or a similar garage sale organizer, so that you can keep track of how much you spent for each item you bought, when you bought it, and how much you sold it for. You will also want to keep track of extra expenses like gas, meals, item cleaning supplies, and packaging supplies, too. You need to know how much money you are actually making, not just the per item profit. You can write off many of these expenses on your income taxes, as well.

6. Start **gathering packaging materials** and boxes! If you sell used goods online, you are going to have to package lots of breakable items. Everything that you don't have to buy saves you money. This can add up to hundreds of dollars a year, by the time that you are selling several thousand items. Start saving sturdy boxes and packing peanuts, bubble wrap, and Styrofoam when you get items in the mail, or when you buy items from stores. Have your friends and neighbors do the same. Get on the USPS website and order a selection of Priority Mail boxes and envelopes. They are totally free, with no shipping fees, so order different sizes and shapes, and also order some flat rate padded envelopes and boxes. I have not had to buy shipping boxes in 12 years of selling, besides specially sized 12 x 12" vinyl record shippers. The rest of the

boxes were free. You WILL have to buy padding materials, especially bubble wrap. Buy the 12" wide, perforated rolls of wrap. Buy them on eBay in bulk and you will save yourself a lot of money.

7. Make sure that you have a **functioning digital camera, and high-speed internet** is well worth the cost, if you have to upgrade from dial-up. You can also write the business portion of your high-speed internet service off on your income taxes.

MOTIVATION AND PRACTICALITY, PLEASE!

My wife and I started flipping garage sale finds and used items 12 years ago, as a supplemental income. We sold vintage collectible items and antiquarian books that we found (95% of the items were 25 cents or less) on eBay for $5-200. That's quite a profit margin, eh?

As more and more people starting selling vintage items on eBay, we looked for other ways to diversify. We expanded into selling primarily media items, as they are easy to store and to ship, and the profit margins are excellent. We bought from a variety of sources, including second-hand stores, sales, book sales, and online at eBay and Craigslist.

We built our modest start into an eBay and **Amazon inventory of over $40,000, along with selling $200-500 a week**. Our garage sale and thrift shop flipping has allowed my wife to stay at home with our two children, instead of working at a traditional job. I built this garage sale business while working a demanding full-time job and having two small children to cart around to Little League games, soccer, and the like.

The moral of this story is: If we can make money flipping garage sale finds, SO CAN YOU.

- You ARE going to have to work. This gig is just like any other home-based business. YOU CAN MAKE

MONEY, but it's not going to be automatic, or given to you. You are going to have to research items to buy at garage sales, until you get good at recognizing the best stuff to buy.

- You are going to have to put in the time learning how to effectively sell items on the internet. This is going to be your business. If you want to succeed, you are going to have to motivate yourself to succeed.

- If you want to make good money, you are going to have to work harder and be smarter than your competition. Remember, there are a lot of unemployed people right now, and eBay reselling can be done by anybody, anywhere. So, you are going to have to beat out your competition. There have thousands and thousands of people who have tried to earn a consistent income selling used items and failed. They failed because they did not have the motivation and knowledge to succeed. If you read this book all the way through and choose a niche that suits you, you *will* have the knowledge and motivation to succeed. You will only have to get out there and go for it!

Well, what are you waiting for?! Let's get ready to roll!

WHERE TO SELL YOUR USED ITEMS

Before you start accumulating used items and materials to sell, it is important to know where you are going to sell them to earn the highest profits. Finding the good stuff to sell is only half of the battle.

In many cases, the quickest way to sell used items is to sell them on eBay. While the sales prices on many collectible items have come down recently due to selling competition on the site, there is always going to be a market for items that people need. eBay is a versatile location where you can sell a large variety of items. Almost anything can be sold for good profits on eBay, if you know which categories to list your items in.

Listing items in the correct category seems like it should be automatic, but many times it is not! There are many items that can be listed in multiple categories, and often only one those categories will allow you to consistently sell your product. You must research completed auctions to know for sure which categories to list your item in.

Just about anything you can think of that is bought and sold in any physical marketplace is also sold one. We will get further in depth into the world of eBay in later chapters, but just realize for now that eBay gives you the best opportunity to diversify your sales, and the potential for buyers to bid higher on items than you may have thought the item was worth to begin with.

Just last summer, we stopped at a garage sale near our house. My wife did the quick loop around the sale, and "Nope, nothing here. All junk."

And, I thought she was right. We were walking out, and I happened to notice a box of old papers underneath a table. Nothing had prices on it. I found an old ratty-looking paperback book, and a couple of other pamphlets. I asked the host how much she wanted for the books, and she said "That one book is $1 because it's really old. You can have the other stuff."

"Cool!" I said.

I handed her a dollar, and when I got back to the car, I looked at the stuff closer. The book was a collection of Creole recipes from New Orleans. It also had some really nice illustrations and vintage advertisements. When I got home, I took photos of the book, plus several of the recipes and ads. I listed the book on eBay and several of the smaller books on Amazon for almost $50. They were rare books from the early 1920s.

Despite having heavy cover damage, the Creole book sold for almost $100 on eBay. If it would have been in better condition, who knows what the final price would have been. Not bad for a garage sale that at first glance appeared to having nothing of value. It just takes some experience, honing your "picking eye", and being out there picking to find this stuff. I have had similar incidents occur frequently.

I have probably found several hundred items that ended up selling for over $50 online that were either free, or priced under $1 at garage sales and thrifts. Most of those items were NOT where the item should have been displayed at the garage sale or thrift store. In other words, the host or thrift store employee had no idea of the value of the item. You have to know you stuff, and understand how to find these types of items when you are picking.

Here are some yard sale tips to help you have more fun and find more valuable stuff at garage sales, yard sales, and estate sales:

1. Check your newspaper classified ads and Craigslist garage sale ads on Thursday. Make a route that allows you to cover the most ground, and spend the least possible amount of gas money. Allow time for a breakfast or lunch break at your favorite affordable restaurant.

2. Get going early! Many of the best deals are gone in the first half hour of the sale opening. Start your day at the garage sale that had the most enticing ad when you made your list on Thursday.

3. Take a friend or relative. It makes the day more enjoyable when you can talk to somebody when you are in the car in between sales, at lunch, etc.

4. Be friendly with the yard sale host. You might make a new friend, and you will definitely be more likely to be able to negotiate prices if you have made a positive impression with the host before you try to talk "business" with them.

5. Take a pocketful of change with you, and some one dollar bills. There are a lot of sales where you will just want to be able to drop a quarter on the table on the way out, instead of waiting for change. This also helps with negotiations. If you are holding a dollar bill in your hand when you say, "I've got these 6 items that you have a

quarter each on, would you take $1 for all of them?", they will be more likely to grab the dollar bill. If they have to make change for a $5, they will often say no.

SELLING ON EBAY AND AMAZON

There are many people who love garage sale and thrift sale shopping, and would love to sell their finds for profits. But, they are either too lazy to make listings on eBay for their finds, or they are intimidated by the process of selling online.

Chances are, readers of this book are NOT going to be too lazy. You made the effort to locate this book, and have read into the book far enough to get this point, so you showing initiative.

However, there are probably some readers who are hesitant to sell online. Perhaps they have not had good luck selling on eBay, or they have friends that failed. Maybe, they have never sold anything online, and have limited computer skills.

If you are any of these people, don't worry about it! We were ALL there at some point. I remember the first time that I came home with stuff to sell. I had boxes sitting on the floor by the computer (which was a large desktop computer, back then), and I thought to myself, "OK, now what?"

I just made myself do it. I went on the eBay site (I did not know about Amazon then), and waded through the Selling Tutorial. I took some photos of my items, and listed the first item within 15 minutes.

If you have never listed an item on eBay, DON'T BE NERVOUS. Just get on the site, and follow the directions. Anybody, and I mean anybody, can easily list items on eBay. Remember, eBay wants everybody to be able to use their site effectively so they can make money on listing and closing fees when you sell there. They have excellent tutorials that take you through the entire selling process. The directions are purposefully designed so that a twelve-year old without computer skills can follow the directions and list an item. You CAN list items on eBay, even if you have never been on the site before. It is really freaking easy.

Selling used items on Amazon is also very easy and I have found that it is more profitable than selling items on eBay for a wide variety of items. Many people think that you can only list used books and media items on Amazon. But, that is not true. You can sell almost any used item on Amazon, and items often sell for significantly higher prices than the same item would sell for on eBay.

Amazon also has excellent tutorials for listing items on their site. It is even easier to sell an item on Amazon than it is to make an auction on eBay.

All you have to do is register to be a seller on the Amazon marketplace. The blue link to the left is an excellent place to start. It tells you about all of the details about selling on Amazon, and provides a link to sign up.

Becoming a seller on Amazon is free. There are no fees to sign up, unless you decide to be a Professional level seller, right off the bat. By signing up to be a Professional seller, you are given the ability to make your own item pages, which are not already in the Amazon Marketplace. I use this frequently for rare music items and used items without bar codes. The professional accounts also do not have to pay a $1 closing fee, which is charged to every item sold under the free account. The Professional selling account costs $39.95 per month. So, when you get to the point that you will be selling at least 40 items a month, you will want to upgrade to the Professional account.

I recommend getting your feet wet by starting with the free account. Build your inventory, and then upgrade to the Professional account after several months.

The best aspects of selling on Amazon are the ease of listing items, and having ZERO listing fees. While eBay charges a minimum of ten cents per item to list an item (even if it does not sell), Amazon lets you list thousands of items for FREE. You can build a large inventory of high priced items, which will continually produce money every month, without paying to list the items.

We have a lot more information on the basics of selling on Amazon and eBay on our website and in *Almost Free Money*, so we will move on to some tips on increasing profits on both sites. If you are new to selling, please check out our website. It has entire pages devoted to background information on the sites, the advantages of each site, packaging items, and shipping items sold on both sites.

INCREASING PROFITS ON EBAY AND AMAZON

There is no doubt that the best way to increase online selling profits is just to get out there and sell some items. See what works for you, and what does not. Every selling situation is a bit different, and different things work well for different sellers.

Having said that, there are three overlying things that every seller can do to increase profits, regardless of their selling niche(s):

1) Research

I'm not sure how many times that I have said this now, but I am sure that I will say it again. Knowing what people are looking for and how to sell those items effectively is paramount to making money in this business. You HAVE to spend the time researching to gain the knowledge necessary to beat out your competition. You must be able to find items that other people miss, and you have to know how to sell items more efficiently and more effectively than other sellers.

I do 90% of my research between 8PM and 1AM, after the kids are in bed. I will not sacrifice my time with my family to make extra profits, but I will divide my attention between my

TV and my laptop computer! I often look for new sources of income, new ways of selling used items, and read eBay seller forums while I am watching the Detroit Tigers games. That's what commercial breaks are for (that and getting snacks and beverages)!

2. **Think like your customers!**

This is very important, yet many internet sellers miss the boat, when it comes to addressing the needs of potential buyers through their eBay auctions or Amazon listings. You have to be able to look at your used items as if you were going to buy them. What would you want to know about that item? What aspects of the item would you want to see photographs of to identify the item and ensure that it was in good enough condition to buy?

Make sure that the concerns of your customers are addressed within your listings. Think to yourself: "What questions would I have about this item, if I was going to buy it?" Then, address those questions through text descriptions or additional photographs.

Many sellers provide only one photo for an eBay auction, and write woefully short and worthless descriptions. You do not need to be a poet to write a good description. All you have to do is completely describe the item (full name of the item, when it was made, and who made it), describe why a buyer would want the item (cool features of the item), and talk about condition of the item. Make sure that all condition defects are noted and photographed. Keep your customers happy, and they will leave you good feedback, so that future buyers will bid on your items.

3. **Don't be Lazy**.

The people that work the hardest make the most money. Isn't that true of most things in life? The same thing applies to internet selling. Spend time doing your research. Take additional photographs, and make your text descriptions complete and appealing. It's easy to skimp on photos and shorten descriptions when you have a lot of items to get listed at one time. But, the time spent making quality listings will directly earn you money. It will also build a group of return customers, which is huge. Sellers should go above and beyond what customers usually experience when buying on eBay and Amazon in order to keep them coming back to you.

Keep those three things in mind, and you will increase your profits dramatically.

For almost a year, I flipped items that I found on eBay, and I made very good money. I looked for items that did NOT observe the three rules above. I found many items for .99 and sold quite a few of those same items for $40-100, just by working harder than the original sellers. I would bid on the items, which were often listed in the wrong categories, had terrible photographs, inadequate titles, or all of the above. When I received the items, I would clean up the surfaces, take multiple photographs, and research where the items should be listed. Then, I would auction the item, or put it on Amazon, and regularly make 20-40X what I paid for the item, just by understanding how to sell the item and working harder than my competition.

And, just for you readers, here are some specific tips that will directly make you more money on eBay and Amazon:

1. eBay: MAKE PEOPLE CLICK ON YOUR ITEM FROM THE CATEGORY LIST. Whenever people do a search for a specific term, or search in a particular category, they are provided a large vertical list of items under that search term. Your item will be listed with up to 200 other listings. You must make people want to click on your item from that list, or you will NOT get bids. How is that accomplished? There are only TWO THINGS that get people to click on your listing to review your item and potentially bid on it: **The Title and the Thumbnail photograph.**

2. eBay: **Make your title interesting**! This is the one thing that I have gotten good at over twelve years that has allowed me to increase my profits the most. It is important to accurately describe your item in the title, but it is more important that your listing stands out in the list of auctions in a search.

Spice up your title. Know what terms other successful listings have used that led customers to bid on them. Research completed listings and look for words that are in many high-yielding auctions that are similar to your item. For instance, use hip words like "Vintage", "Mid-Century", or "Retro" to describe items, instead of dry words like "old", or "antique". Words like vibrant, colorful, and unique catch people's eye. Words like "scarce" and "rare" are used constantly by sellers, and many bidders avoid auctions with those words in the titles.

eBay recently allowed more characters to be used in the item titles. Use that to your advantage, but do not clutter up you titles with worthless junk words. Make sure that your keywords and action words stand out by placing them at the beginning of the titles. Do not make your title look gaudy by using all caps.

3. eBay: Make your Cover Photo eye-catching.

The thumbnail photograph that is used along with the title is very important. You know the old saying about pictures and 1,000 words. The trick on eBay is to make a very small photo relevant, especially for many items that really are not that exciting, such as old books with no dust jackets.

There are many tricks that can be learned just by looking at completed item listings. What catches YOUR eye, when you are skimming completed listings? Use what you like. One easy tip is to use contrasting colors and bright backgrounds to make boring items stand out. One of the rooms in our house is a dark maroon color, which I use as a contrast for light colored items. Another wall is lime green, which makes a great background for dark colored items. You can also use textures to stand out, such as using velvet or corduroy fabric took take photos on.

4. Amazon: Instill buyer confidence with your item description. Let people know that you know what you are doing. Accurately describe your item using the lingo that collectors use (e.g. terms like dust jacket and FFEP for books). I also add a sentence at the end of the description about securely packing items in bubble wrap and fast shipping. Make your listing stand out from the others. Once you develop a wording in your listings, you can cut-and-paste the same description template for each item, and only change the item and condition.

5. eBay and Amazon: Be very familiar with Shipping Costs and Packaging:

You can save a lot of money by using the correct shipping services. We use USPS. Yes, they damage more items than UPS or FedEx, but they are also cheaper. They will also pick up packages at your home or business for free, as long as you have at least one Priority Mail package.

You have to know how much an item is going to cost before you list it! Don't throw away profits by undercharging for shipping fees, because you were too lazy to weigh your item and figure out the shipping cost. By understanding shipping options, you can also maximize your profits. The more a customer has to pay for shipping fees on eBay, the lower the ending price of your item will be. If your item qualifies for Media Mail shipping, offer it. Many sellers only offer Priority Mail shipping because they get free Priority boxes from the USPS, but the shipping cost prevents potential bidders from bidding on their items.

Packaging supplies are also important to ensuring safe arrival of customers' items, and sellers should include the costs of packaging items in the shipping cost quoted. It may only be a quarter for packaging cost per item, but that .25 adds up over hundreds of packages shipped. We have a lot more information on packing and shipping eBay and Amazon items on Garage Sale Academy.com.

GARAGE SALES SHOPPING

Finding stuff to make large profits on at garage sales used to be easy. Now, there are many people re-selling items from garage sales online.   In addition, the people hosting the garage sales are more aware of the value of many collectible items than they used to be. Still, you can find many great items to sell at yard sales, often for very cheap prices. You can regularly find $10-20 items for under a dollar. How's that for profit?

Here are a number of tips to help you find stuff at garage sales to sell:

Number one, do your homework ahead of time.   Go through the newspaper classifieds and Craigslist to find sales that advertise what you like to sell, or similar items. Write down when the sales start and end, and what they are supposed to have at the sale that you are interested in. Look for sales that advertise large bunches of stuff, '25 years of accumulation', or that type of language in the ad.

Make every effort to be at the most attractive sale first when it opens. If you can go to sales on Fridays, you can find much more material to sell than if you wait until the sale has been running for a day or two on Saturday morning.   Make yourself a route that hits all of the good sales.   This prevents you from wasting time and gas money by going back and forth across the county to get to all of the garage sales.   If you can hit a neighborhood or citywide sale, start there.

Number two, don't mess around at yard sales. Treat your inventory picking as a business. It is fun to shop at garage sales, but you are there for a reason. Say hello to the homeowner, but don't talk to them for half an hour. If you get to the tables, and there is nothing of value, move on to the next sale.

If you do find items that you want to buy, ask if you can stack them by the pay table. Get what you are going to get at the sale, pay, and leave.   This allows you to hit the most sales possible in the time that you have for that day.

Number three, look at EVERYTHING at the garage sale. This may seem to contradict rule number two, but it really doesn't. When you get more experienced hitting sales, you will understand exactly what I mean. Don't waste time talking and wandering around.   Ensure you look at all the tables at the sale. I have found tons of great items underneath junk on tables, inside other boxes, scattered in amongst books, in boxes of toys, and everywhere else that you can think of. The items you are looking for are items that the seller does NOT know the value of.   This stuff could be anywhere at the sale.

As a matter of fact, I have found some of my best items in FREE boxes or 5 or 10 cent boxes, thrown in with a bunch of junk. If you see these types of boxes ALWAYS look in them all the way to the bottom of the box. If it's a free box, you can always grab the whole box to save time, and go through it later. You are doing the homeowner a favor by getting rid of the box of junk for them. Take almost any books, CDs, DVDs, or media items that you see in a free box. I have found multiple $50 books in free boxes at sales.

As a savvy reseller, you also have the advantage of having an Amazon selling account. This puts you ahead of 95% of the re-sellers you are competing with at garage sales, who are only selling on eBay. Look for media items that you can sell for a higher price on Amazon, as well as boxed items with bar codes that you can resell. Make sure you quickly grab anything sealed in shrink wrap that you can sell as 'New'.

Number four may be the most important rule. Make sure that you can sell the items that you are picking up. Condition is one of the most important things to consider when deciding on whether to buy an item. Is the item operational? Does it have all the parts? Does it need additional cords or parts to be able to sell them?

Plug electronic items in to test them. Almost everybody has outdoor outlets available to test with. If they refuse to let you test an item, don't buy it. It probably does not work.

Also, keep in mind that some items are valuable without being functional. You just have to remember that you are going to have to spend additional money for parts, plus spend time fixing the item, which cuts into your profit.

For instance, it is quite common to find vintage video game systems without cords. That does not mean that you should not buy the systems, if the price is right. It is very easy to get cords online for any video game system, and they are usually fairly cheap. You can also save the systems for a while and try to find cords at other sales, or at thrift stores.

Make sure that you examine the entire item. Does it have broken corners or re-glued pieces? Is it missing accessories? The collectible value of the item is going to be significantly reduced if there are major condition issues.

Also, keep in mind the shipping cost of heavy items. There are many collectible items that would make nice profits, if it was not for the weight of the item. Figure on all items over one pound to cost over $5 in shipping costs, plus an extra $2+ for every pound after that. A heavy metal item could easy cost your potential winning bidder on eBay an additional $15 in shipping fees on top of their winning bid. Consider the total cost that you think the average collector would pay for an item.

Large items are difficult and time-consuming to package, and you also have to pay for bubble wrap to prevent damage. So, many large or heavy items appear to be good money makers, but they end up breaking even after allowing for shipping costs.

Number five, keep a magnet in your pocket for identifying valuable scrap metals such as copper, brass, and silver-plate. Remember that non-magnetic metals are usually more valuable than the metal objects that stick to your magnet.

FREE TREASURE TO SELL AT GARAGE SALES!

I would say that about 60% of garage sales and yard sales will have free stuff that is there for anybody to latch onto. The host is simply looking to get rid of some of their worthless junk. However, it is not very often that there is nothing of value in the free boxes of any garage sale. I have found hundreds of dollars of treasure in free boxes over the years!

Free boxes will often be out by the road, or at the beginning of the tables. Don't be afraid to grab the whole free box, and go through it later. After all, you are doing the garage sale host a favor by removing the box for them.

I often feel guilty about plundering free gold at garage sales, and at least make sure to buy something small from the yard sale. I often find several $20 items in free boxes. I think that I can spare a quarter or two to thank the host.

Dig through the all of the contents of the box, all the way to the bottom. I have dug through trash, and found lots of treasure at the bottom of free boxes: $40 books, new CDs worth $30, a working Gameboy system, many portable video game cartridges, vinyl records worth $40, a 24K gold necklace, other gold and silver jewelry, very old post cards, stamps, vintage marbles, baseball cards, and all kinds of "broken" vintage electronics that were easily fixed!

Remember, many broken vintage electronics can be parted out and sold for excellent money. Many large items have parts that can be sold, because the parts in these old systems often fail. Collectors also like to customize their systems with parts from other vintage electronics.

WHAT TO LOOK FOR IN FREE BOXES

1. Books: I have found many collectible books in free boxes. Look for softcover text books, they also regularly bring $10-20. Books are great because they can be listed on Amazon in several seconds, and they do not take up much room in your storage area.
2. Movies: Any DVDs, and some VHS tapes.
3. CDs, Cassettes, Vinyl Records. List these items on Amazon.
4. Knick-knacks, curios, and decorative collectibles
5. Vintage holiday decorations
6. Video Games, Cases, and Manuals
7. Remote Controls (Any). If you see remote controls, take them. These often get lost and

people replace them by buying them online. I have sold quite few vintage remotes for electronics and toys on Amazon for over $15. You can even sell the battery compartment doors, in some cases.

8. Computer accessories, especially old collectible items from Apple II, Commodore, etc.

9. Video Game accessories like controllers, power cords, AV cords, etc. You never know when you will find a system at a garage sale that is missing a cord. The accessories also sell well online on Amazon.

10. Vintage electronics and components.

11. Scrap Metal. Anything large and metal should go in your truck or trailer. Remember, every time you get a truckload of scrap metal, you will earn $160. Also pull out anything with a power cord. They have good scrap value. Many old computers and vintage electronics contain gold and silver in their interiors

12. Remove anything that might be gold plated, silver plated, solid copper, or solid brass. You should always have a magnet with you when you pick. Precious metals do not stick to a magnet. This is the real free gold at garage sales.

13. Paper items like stamps, old mailings with stamps attached, trading cards, and vintage playing cards

14. Small toys like vintage Matchbox and Hot Wheels cars, action figures, Legos, and other collectible toys.

THRIFT SHOPS

Thrift shops can be great locations to find items to resell. They are the leftovers from hundreds of garage sales all in one location! Often, families also drop off their items at thrift stores because they do not have the time to host a garage sale. Many used items at thrifts have never been offered for sale. Save yourself gas money and pick used items at thrift stores like Goodwill and Salvation Army.

There are advantages and disadvantages to re-selling from thrift stores and second-hand stores.

First, the advantages:

There is a large accumulation of items at thrifts! Many people do not have the time or inclination to hold their own garage sale, so they give away boxes of their used goods to Goodwill stores for a tax break. Instead of looking at one or two family's stuff at a garage sale, you can sift through hundreds of family's stuff at one second-hand store!

Instead of driving to many yard sales, and spending your gas money, you can drive to one or two thrift stores and see the same amount of items, or maybe even more.

Prices at second hand stores are still relatively low. They are generally higher than prices you will see at most garage sales, but still much lower than if you were to go to a collectibles store, or if you were looking online. There are usually profits to be made. You just have to know where to find the best items to resell. Many thrift store items are priced by people who are not making direct profits from the sale of the items.

In other words, if thrift store employees price a board game at $1 and it sells, the employee does not make $1, like a garage sale host does. You can find great deals, if you are present at the thrift shop when a new item is placed on the shelf for sale!

Thrift stores are not weather dependent like yard sales. They have set hours and days that they are open. You can shop there whenever they are open, which makes it much more convenient for pickers with 9-5 jobs. Most thrift stores are open at least until 7PM.

If you resell in a particular category of items, you can concentrate your search and find a lot of items to resell quickly, especially if your selling niche is used media, used clothing, children's toys, or household items.

And now, for the disadvantages:

You have a lot more competition at thrift shops than at garage sales. While resellers are spread out over a multitude of yard sales on weekends, second-hand stores are convenient locations that most internet sellers frequent.

Prices are usually going to be higher than at garage sales. This is especially true of media items. Books at Goodwill stores usually run 35 to 70 cents for paperbacks and $1-2 for hardcovers. You either have to have a Smartphone with a price checker or be very confident that the book is a high value book to consistently make good profits. The same is true of CDs and LP records. You can often find books for 10 cents for paperbacks, and 50 cents for hardcovers at garage sales. CDs and records can often be found for 10 to 25 cents each at yard sales, instead of $1-2 at thrift stores.

There are more broken items at thrifts, including items with missing pieces, and CDs and records with mismatched covers. Double check all items that you are considering buying before you pay for them! Always check to make sure that CDs are not missing from inside the cases, and records are in the jackets. Board games are also often missing pieces, but thrift stores often tape the boxes shut, so it can be difficult to check them. Sometimes, you just have to take a chance. Most second hand stores will allow you to return items, but it costs you time and gas money to do so.

You usually cannot haggle on prices at thrifts, like you can at rummage sales.

Some chain thrift shops have internet listings or auctions for their collectible items. That means they have employees at those locations that are looking for the collectible items that resellers would otherwise be able to find on the store shelves. Obviously, there are going to be fewer gold nuggets at these locations.

TIPS FOR MAKING MONEY AT THRIFTS

Since there is more competition at thrift shops, you have to work harder and be more knowledgeable than everybody else:

- If your local thrifts have a 50% off tag color, like Goodwill stores, be at the thrift store when it opens on the day that the tag colors change.
- Get to know your local thrift store owners and managers. Give them your business cell phone number and email address, or a business card. Tell them you will give them some money for their unsold media items or items in your selling niche(s). You may also be able to leave them a box to put their broken items in. Then you can sell components from the items, or fix them and resell them. You can also make good money on the scrap metal value of broken vintage electronics.
- Some great items that you can find at many thrift shops: Used Books and Media, board games, factory-sealed items (which should be sold on Amazon), vintage clothing, suits and high-end dresses, vintage T-shirts, holiday decorations, vintage audio, vintage reel to reel, Sterling Silver and plated gold, collectible costume jewelry, vintage shoes and handbags, and copper and brass for scrap metal value.

- The more you shop and buy items from thrift shops, the better you will get at finding the best deals with the highest profits. If you stay at it, you WILL find $50 items for under $3, and you WILL also lose money on some items. It is all part of the game. You cannot win on every purchase.
- Don't bother with any items that you can't make at least $5 profit on. It takes too long to prepare and list auctions on eBay to make it worth your while, if you are not making a minimum of $5.
- By reselling on both eBay and Amazon, you have a leg up on many other internet sellers. There are huge advantages to listing particular items on each website, and there are many internet sellers that only list on eBay, or Amazon sellers dealing solely in used media.

FLEA MARKETS

Flea Market flipping and shopping success depends on you being more knowledgeable than your competition. In this chapter, we will provide some tips to find some great hidden treasures at flea markets.

Probably the biggest advantage to picking at these locations instead of at garage sales or yard sales is that at flea markets, items are much better organized. For instance, if you like looking for a particular category of collectibles like glassware, vinyl records, or vintage toys, you are likely going to be able to find an entire vendor that specializes in that type of collectible.

Introduce yourself to vendors that sell the items that you are interested in. These people are constantly shopping for inventory to resell. If they have your contact information, they can get a hold of you if they find what you like!

Unless you like throwing away money, you should always be able to barter to get a lower price than what is on the price sticker. Vendors are similar to used car salesmen. They bought their items to resell, and they have to make a profit on them. But, just like cars at a used car lot, all items have some "wiggle room" built into their prices. Vendors WILL deal with you on most prices. If they don't, move on to the next vendor!

Remember that vendors are not garage sale hosts. They are not selling their items just to get them out of their house, like garage sale hosts are. They are selling the items only to make a profit. They usually have a good idea how much collectibles are worth.

Be prepared to spend a little bit more for individual items at flea markets than at yard sales, but keep it in perspective. If you know that you can find similar items at yard sales for considerably lower prices, you may want to pass on those types of items when you see them at flea markets. Advertising collectibles would be one example of items that are always overpriced at flea markets.

Flea markets can be great spots to accessorize your garage sale finds. You can often find the power cords or controllers for video game systems that you previously found at thrift stores or garage sales, but were missing cords. You can also find remotes for vintage audio components, upgrade vinyl record jackets for high-end records, find stylus needles for record players, complete sports card sets, and make larger collections of decorative items to resell.

If you like a high priced item, make an offer! You never know when the vendor will want to deal. Maybe that item has been sitting in his booth for years, and he is tired of seeing it!

FLIPPING FLEA MARKET ITEMS

The flipping of flea market items can be tougher than at garage sales, yard sales and thrift stores. Vendors are actually your competition. They often have their own internet auctions or listings. They are not just "picking opportunities" for you, they are your rival.

I do not tell vendors that I resell items. I find that they are more likely to agree to my offers, if they think that the item will be not resold. It is not a lie to tell vendors that you are a collector. You just choose to sell some of the items that you "collect", right?

Flipping at flea markets is tough, but rewarding. Think of it as a challenge to make money off of these vendors and their items. Anybody can make money from garage sale finds, but it takes knowledge and work to make good money from flea market items.

Use the knowledge gained from "Fast Cash" and "Almost Free Money" to make money from imperfect items. You can make good money by parting out broken vintage items for components, for instance. You can also easily fix many items for resale.

Vendors often price their items by looking at fellow vendors' items or by using old outdated price guides. You can make good money buying items that are 'Hot' on eBay and Amazon, or items that are desirable in other regions of the country or in foreign countries.

Look for college and sports memorabilia that can be sold better online than locally. The local sports teams will always be highly priced at nearby flea markets, but you can find good deals on popular teams from farther away. I have found some excellent deals on football jerseys, sports cards, pennants, and artwork for teams that the vendors' local customers were not interested in. The local teams' stuff will usually be too highly priced to make money on.

RESEARCH

If there is one area that a motivated seller will stand out above their competition, it is in their knowledge base relating to the items they sell.   Start with what you are familiar with, and then expand your knowledge from there.

You do not have to know much to sell usable items, clothing, and other non-collectible items online.   You only have to identify the item in an auction or on the Amazon marketplace, describe the condition, and then make it available for purchase.

However, other items such as collectibles, high-end electronics, computer equipment, and auto parts require the seller to have background knowledge before selling the item. In order to be able to describe the item sufficiently so that a potential buyer is comfortable buying it from you, the seller has to understand what type of information the buyer needs for them to determine value and functionality.

Start selling what you know the best. If you grew up collecting sports cards and memorabilia, and you have boxes of baseball cards in your closet, start by selling your excess cards.   You already know how to describe baseball cards to potential buyers. You can 'speak the language' to card collectors on eBay.

Get yourself a current price guide so that you have an idea of the current market value. Then, gather a number of cards that you are interested in selling and type the player's name and year of the sport card in the search bar on eBay. Click on the checkbox on the left side of the screen that says 'Completed Listings'. You get a list of the ended auctions from the last three months with your search description. The average ending price is what you should expect to sell your card for, if the condition is also similar.

The same process can be applied to any subject area. When you have an item that you want to determine value on, take a look at the last three months of sales on eBay. You should be able to make a quick determination if the item is worth your time. If you are considering selling the item on Amazon, locate the item in the Amazon marketplace using the search bar, and see what the average price listed is.

eBay completed listings can also help you in other ways. Let's say that you found a vintage Pioneer audio receiver for free at a garage sale. Good for you! Now, how do you make a profit on it, if you have never dealt with electronics before?

If you plug it in and everything works, you just hit the jackpot. Look on the back of the unit and find the model number. Type it into the search bar, and see what similar working units have sold for, and list your receiver starting at the low end of the completed listing's end prices. You want to encourage bidders by starting at what feels like a bargain to the bidder.

If you attempt to test the receiver and it doesn't work at all, don't worry. You actually may make more money by disassembling the receiver and selling the parts.

The trick is to determine which components and parts to sell. You should have an idea what parts are going to be sold BEFORE taking the receiver apart, because some larger components are more valuable whole then totally disassembled. For instance, if your vintage audio item has a record player, you will want to keep the entire tone-arm assembly together to sell it.

In order to determine what we are going to sell, we use Completed Listings again. Type in the model number from the receiver on the main eBay page. Most of the time, the search will return many whole receivers that were for sale. But, it will also give you a list of parts and components that other sellers have listed and what the ending prices were.

For instance, with vintage Pioneer receivers, you would probably find that the outer case was worth listing (and would make you some good money, if it was wood). You would also note that the knobs, feet, emblem, and face plate were worth money. Usually the tuning mechanism, display, and some of the internal workings will also be listed.

You may also want to go to the 'Vintage Electronics' category and look at the Completed Listings for the entire category. This will give you a general idea of some of the parts that are often valuable, regardless of brand. You would probably note that large power transformers are usually worth money, and since your Pioneer has a similar transformer to the ones that you saw in Completed Listings, you would want to list your own transformer in the category that you found the others in.

A good seller is curious. If you are at a garage sale, you should be looking for new sources of income. If you find something interesting, look it up in Completed Listings when you get home, and see if it's worth your time.

I spend a lot of time just browsing Completed Listings in given categories and looking for new areas to list items in. If I find an interesting listing that did really well for another seller, I look at the auction page and try to figure out why it did better than others in the same category. Were there certain words used in the item title? Were the photos showing a certain aspect of the item? Was the item described in a particular way? If I can pick up anything useful, I use similar wordings in my titles or descriptions.

You may also find totally new areas to sell items in. I remember one night browsing Completed Listings to see if any 1980s-era magazines were worth buying at garage sales, because I was seeing them quite often. I found that 95% of the magazines I was seeing were not going to be worth the time it took to list them. But, I saw some listings in other categories that *were* interesting.

Other sellers were <u>listing just the advertisements from magazines and newspapers for good money</u>. Often, the magazines the ads came from could be found for $1, but the ads within could be worth up to $20 apiece. People were looking for ads containing celebrities or certain products (like vintage autos, or Atari 2600 games) and framing them for décor in their homes and businesses.

So I picked up a bunch of magazines, and clipped interesting ads out. I scanned the ads with my scanner, and listed them on eBay. I made several hundred dollars selling magazine ads in a relatively short time. I looked at a number of sellers'

51

listings, and it was apparent that they sold only magazine ads and did quite well.

I sold ads for a while, but I quickly realized that you have to make a lot of listings to make any real money, and I found it quite monotonous clipping and scanning, so I moved on to more interesting ventures. If you are interested in selling ads, there are books available on Amazon for identifying and pricing print ads to get you started. The startup cost is almost zero, and you will make some money if you can find some older magazines to pull ads from.

SELLING SCRAP METAL: MINIMIZING LOSS IN THE FAST CASH SYSTEM

One of the most unique and profitable aspects of the *Fast Cash* and *Almost Free Money* systems is the selling of scrap metal. Honestly, I am not sure why this has not been used before these books, but I have never seen the combination of internet selling and selling scrap metal in any other books. I have no idea why.

Selling scrap metal is incredibly easy. All you have to do is throw a bunch of metal junk into a pickup truck, and haul it to a scrap metal dealer. They will pay you $150, and they will even remove the metal for you, in most cases!

The process of selling scrap metal is no more difficult than selling used items on the internet. Once you do it once, you've got it. Then, everything else is easy money (Fast Cash, baby!) Also, as you learn more about scrapping and high-profit scrap metal, you can enhance your scrap metal profits by selling the good stuff – gold, silver, and platinum. You can also learn how to find high-value materials that nobody else is looking for, like carbide steel drill bits. This is covered in detail, with about four chapters in *Almost Free Money*, so just the basics will be covered in *Fast Cash*.

In order to effectively use the sale of scrap metal to minimize internet sales losses in the *Fast Cash* system, you have to a basic understanding of what types of metals can be sold. Everybody knows that truck-loads of mixed metal and steel can be hauled to a scrap metal dealer, and sold. As noted earlier, a full load of mixed metal will earn you somewhere in the area of $150-180. So, if you do nothing more than save unsold metal items in a pile, and then haul them to the scrap metal dealer periodically, you can easily make over $100 a year.

This is also a great way to augment your internet sales. Just by picking up metal junk along your garage sale route or free items at the sales themselves, you could easily haul several loads of metal to the dealer at $150 a pop.

By doing some additional research into scrap metal, you can learn many additional items to look for while you are picking used items for resale. Many of these materials can be sold either at your local scrap metal dealer, or you can sell them on eBay. Almost Free Money contains an appendix list that specifies a wide array of these types of materials. Another great spot to start your research is the Scrap Metal Junkie website. A link is provided at the end of this book.

As an appetizer, here are some items that I find all of the time at garage sales and thrifts along with their 2013 values: Car batteries ($5), Power Tool Batteries ($5-50, click on the hyperlink for a great selling opportunity), dead cell phones ($1-80), Empty Printer Cartridges, computer components, copper wires ($1.10/lb), decorative copper items ($3/LB), decorative brass items ($2/LB), Dead Lithium-Ion batteries (.60/LB), aluminum wheels (.80/LB), carbide bits and other high-speed steel, and lots more.

Sometimes, you can even make more on the scrap metal value of large items than you can by selling them online as used collectibles.

Selling scrap metal is an intricate part of the *Fast Cash* system. It adds another income source for sellers, which is dependable, because it has a defined value. Its price is not affected by competition, like collectible items are.

Many items that remain unsold for long periods of time on eBay and Amazon can also be salvaged by selling them as scrap metal, or disassembling them to sell as a combination of scrap metal and components. These smaller components can often be sold easier on eBay than the larger whole units, due to shipping cost issues.

Selling stale items for scrap allows internet sellers to free up room in their storage areas and usually recover the purchase costs of the items.

Scrap metal can also provide large lump sums at the end of each garage sale season. Last year, my family went on a week-long East Coast vacation financed primarily through the sale of the scrap metal that I had collected for less than one year. I had two truck-loads of steel at $350, about $60 in copper, $50 in car batteries, about $50 in copper breakage and electric motors, $30 in brass, and I sold about another $200 in computer scrap on eBay.

IMPLEMENTING THE FAST CASH SYSTEM

I read one thing on an internet guru's site a couple of months ago that has really stuck with me. She said that if you do what other people are unwilling to do for one year, you will be able to do things that other people cannot do for the rest of your life.

That is exactly what the *Fast Cash* system will allow you to do, if you get off your butt and get moving! Fast Cash allows you to start a second income with very low initial costs, and build an inventory that pays you money continually for years.

Here are the keys to successfully implementing the system, and remaining profitable over time.

1) Online research allows you to be flexible over time and regardless of economic situations. Sellers should have a diversity of income sources, and continually search for new and exciting opportunities. Schedule a block of time each week that allows you to research online, even when it is your busy selling season, and allow even more time in the winter, when you are not as busy.

2) By selling on both eBay and Amazon, Fast Cash sellers have a huge advantage. eBay sales allow sellers to make immediate profits so that they have funds to buy more

inventory. eBay is also great for selling rare collectibles and high-end items that will earn more profits by offering them in an auction setting.

Amazon allows sellers to build an inventory for free, and yields constant and reliable income over time. Even when sellers are too busy with the rest of their lives to list eBay items, Amazon will continue to pay out, as customers buy items that were listed months ago. It's awesome when that rare $300 book that you listed in July sells on Amazon just before Christmas. Amazon sales are the gifts that keep on giving. You just have to build your inventory up, and the income grows right with it.

3) Start selling on both sites immediately. Don't wait until you have a whole basement full of stuff before you start listing it. Not only does listing your stuff immediately put money back into your pocket so you can "pick" additional inventory, it also increases your confidence in your buying abilities and gives you a feel for what you should be looking for the next time you pick. Make sure that you list on both sites immediately. Get a feel for what prices you can list items for on Amazon, and see what your eBay auctions are yielding back into your *Fast Cash* system. You should have a good idea what works for you and what does not after several weeks of listing.

4. Don't get frustrated if you are not an immediate success. There is a learning curve associated with picking used items and also with selling them online. Do not expect to be a professional seller overnight. Nobody was, including me. It takes time to perfect your skills, and also to get familiar with

the good stuff through your internet research. The more items that you pick and attempt to sell, the better you will get at spotting items. Your auctions and listings will also improve over time. Savor the great treasures that you find (and you WILL find some almost immediately), and don't linger over the items that do not sell. Nobody sells every one of their items, which is why it is important to be able to recoup some of those losses through the sale of scrap metal and components.

5. Keep at it! Many people give up after a week or two of picking because they did not make $1000 overnight. Well, duh! Of course you didn't, unless you got really lucky. We were all there at one time. The key is to develop your skills and become an expert in your niche(s). Spend the time, and it will pay you back many times over down the line. Do not quit, even if it is hard at first, or not as much fun as you expected. It gets much better, and it gets better quickly, in many cases. There's nothing quite like finding a $100 in a free box. It's quite a thrill!

6. Have fun with your business. The best part about this gig is that it's fun. Instead of picking up a second job waiting on people at a restaurant, you are outside shopping at garage sales!

THANK YOU, READERS!

Thank you for taking the time to read this book. I hope that you enjoyed it as much as I enjoyed researching the background content and putting this book together.

Please put your mind to immediately applying what you learned in *Fast Cash*. DO NOT wait until next week or next month to start! You can find items to sell in any location, and at any time of the year.

YOU have to make up your mind to get the ball rolling, and it will be all downhill from there. I hope that you will have as much fun as my family and I have finding treasure for free, or plucking treasure from garage sales and thrift stores.

If you have any questions, contact me on my <u>Facebook</u> page, at <u>Garage Sale Academy's Forum</u>, on <u>Twitter</u>, or email me at <u>almostfreemoney@yahoo.com</u>. I would like to hear from you!

If you feel that this book has helped you to find new and enjoyable ways to make money or save your family cash, I ask you for only two things. #1, tell your family and friends about this book, and #2, please take several seconds to <u>leave positive feedback regarding this book on its Amazon Detail Page</u>. Positive feedback directly affects other readers' reviews and leads to additional orders, and the proceeds from this book will go directly into my sons' college funds.

WEBSITES AND LINKS

Here are some very helpful websites and web pages to jump-start your research process. These are my favorites, after hundreds of hours surfing the internet (several of these links also appear in *Almost Free Money*):

1. eBay Underground:

This forum provides a ton of information related to internet selling. It leans toward eBay selling, obviously, but also discusses selling on Amazon and general inventory picking tips. You have to sign up to enter, but it is a free site and they do not send any spam emails. I am a member and post here regularly.

2. TreasureNet Forum: Garage Sale Finds:

This is a really cool free forum that discusses all kinds of treasure hunting, from metal detecting to gold hunting. It also has a very nice active forum on garage sale hunting and even finding free stuff by 'dumpster diving'. Not so sure about that one, but there is some interesting and unique information here. I am a member and post in the forum regularly.

3. http://www.scrapmetaljunkie.com/scrap-metal-handbook-guide

I still can't believe this site is free. A tremendous amount of information, and well organized. The site provides a nice explanation on how to sort and identify scrap metals.

This is the only site that I have found that provides step-by-step instructions on how to disassemble appliances and other large items for maximizing scrap metal recovery.

Includes: How to take apart a TV, Computer, Washing Machine, Microwave, and many other items. Also has an excellent blog, with information from many experienced scrappers. Regardless of whether you are a beginner, or an experienced scrapper, if you have not been to this site, you will make money by spending time here.

4. http://boardsort.com

This company will pay you up front through PayPal immediately upon confirmation of your information with digital photo of your material. They pay competitive prices for computer scrap, gold board fingers, and some other related e-scrap. You have to pay for shipping, but they pay up front, which is nice. They also have an updated price list of what they pay for a variety of materials, so you know what you can expect to be paid when you send them your scrap.

5. http://voices.yahoo.com/find-almost-free-gold-thrift-shops-yard-sales-beginner-113530.html?cat=51

Also has a link for finding silver. Good explanation of the different classifications of gold and silver, their markings on jewelry, and how to find it for cheap at garage sale, thrift shops, etc.

6. https://itsdeductibleonline.intuit.com

As discussed in Donations section. Provides IRS-accepted values for your donations, and keeps track of your donations for the entire tax year. Inserts your donations into online Income tax forms such as TurboTax.

7. http://used.addall.com

Free book search with values, used for finding values for rare and collectible books. Save this to your favorites, you should be using this site on a regular basis.

8. http://pulse.ebay.com

Provides a 'Hot List' for EBay completed listings. There is a drop-down box at the top for searching specific categories.

9. http://www.isoldwhat.com

Has entire listing of EBay categories, and also number of individual listings for each category and subcategory. Also has Amazon browse counts by category.

10. http://www.metalprices.com

Spot prices for most precious and scrap metals, plus historical prices, with graphs.

11. Identify Vintage T-Shirts

How to tell a real vintage T-Shirt from a modern reproduction

OTHER BOOKS BY ERIC MICHAEL

<u>Almost Free Money: How to Make Significant Money on Free Items That You Can Find Anywhere, Including Garage Sales, Scrap Metal, and Discarded Items</u> [Kindle Edition]

<u>http://www.amazon.com/Almost-Free-Money-Significant-ebook/dp/B008GPTB92</u>

Almost Free Money provides solutions to all of these problems facing many people in our current economic condition. This 119-page document (which is all information content, and no extraneous illustrations) is a compilation of ten years of research into materials that can **easily be found in any location around the world for free or under $1**. The book teaches readers methods for effectively reselling items online on eBay and at the Amazon marketplace with extremely high profit rates.

Here are the Top Ten Benefits from reading Almost Free Money:

1. Learn how to get your hands on tons of free items and materials that can be sold on the internet from home, or at physical locations if you prefer. **Readers are provided with appendices containing over 520 such items, and the eBay categories where the items may be listed for maximum profit**. Identify items that

already exist in your home that can be sold for great money.

2. We will take a tour through **your home and property** and discuss items that can make you money instantly!

3. **Find gold, silver and platinum for free** in a variety of sources. Gold currently has a spot price of about $1700 a troy ounce.

4. If you are an internet seller, and only selling on eBay, you are missing the boat! You will learn where to effectively sell your treasure.

5. Learn what to look for while you are at **garage sales, thrift stores, and flea markets**.

6. You will learn how to sell scrap metal - the ultimate free money. You will take a virtual trip to a scrap metal dealer. Selling scrap is easy and fun.

7. Launch your home business for peanuts, and organize your business effectively, including record keeping and income tax issues.

8. **Learn how to research** on the internet, the most important skill for an entrepreneur.

9. **Make money from home at any time of the day or night. You will build an inventory and make money while you sleep**.

10. Find inventory **anywhere in the world**.

Almost Free Money [Softcover Book]

http://www.amazon.com/Almost-Free-Money-Significant-Including/dp/1482554968

You will want to have a hard copy with you when you are looking for inventory. You can refer to the 520 item

Appendix list of items found for under $1, and where to list them on eBay. Keep it in your car, or in your handbag!

Garage Sale Superstar: How to Make the Most Money Possible at your Garage Sale, Yard Sale, Rummage Sale, Estate Sale, or Tag Sale [Kindle Edition]

http://www.amazon.com/Garage-Sale-Superstar-Possible-ebook/dp/B00ATKB6K4

Garage Sale Superstar provides solutions to all of these questions asked by almost every single garage sale or yard sale host.

In *Superstar*, the second book in the Almost Free Money series, detailed instructions are provided for making excellent money by selling your used property at free venues like garage sales, yard sales, estate sales, and tag sales.

As a veteran of visiting over 1,000 garage sales in the last ten years, I can provide specific examples of what works for garage sale hosts, and what does not.

Here are the Top Ten Benefits from reading Garage Sale Superstar:

1. Learn garage sale techniques used by the most successful garage sale hosts to rake in thousands of dollars at their personal garage sales.
2. Learn how to maximize your garage sale for either higher profits or more items sold. Determine whether

you want max sales, or clearing clutter to clean out your home or garage.

3. Ensure that you have a SAFE garage sale. You would be surprised how many hosts neglect their family's safety, or the safety of kids visiting their sales.

4. Learn how to arrange your displays and tables, one of the most important aspects of maximizing garage sale and yard sale profits.

5. Make your own free garage sale advertisements that will make people flock to your sale, with zero advertising fees. Learn what to put in your ads, where to post them, and how to spice up your classified ads with photos or graphics.

6. Learn what days of the week to be open, and what hours are peak selling times. What time should your garage sale be open in the morning?

7. We have some innovative ideas for making garage sales inviting to potential shoppers, and passers-by on your street. They are also fun for hosts and their children.

8. Discover what types of items are collectible and should be sold on eBay to make significantly more money.

9. Do you hate the process of organizing your garage sale? Learn how to make it fun by including your friends and family. Organize your garage sale items, while socializing or perhaps over several adult drinks.

10. This works anywhere in the world. Anybody can do this!

APPENDIX 1: THE TOP 10 GARAGE SALE ITEMS TO FLIP

Here is a fun countdown list of the top 10 money making garage sale items for garage sale shoppers and investors to look for and how to sell them on the internet.

We have shopped at thousands of garage sales, and sold over 12,000 garage sale finds on Amazon and eBay. Here are our best sellers:

#10 Scrap Metal

I am amazed by the amount and quality of scrap metal that you can find at garage sales and yard sales! You just have to know what to look for.

Scrap metal is great, because it has a defined value, you don't have to worry about whether it will sell on eBay, and it is quick, easy cash in your pocket. You can also <u>disassemble what other people think is junk, and sell the components on eBay</u>.

9 *Anything New and Sealed*:

This is another often overlooked area of excellent profits. ANYTHING that is new and sealed in the original packaging will bring double or triple the value of the same item that is even lightly used.

Even vintage items that are sealed can be sold as new. <u>Media items</u> like CDs, Movies, and Video Games can even be found still sealed, and they sell like hotcakes.

Almost anything with a barcode can easily be listed and sold on Amazon without a listing fee.

8 *Vintage Electronics:*

Even experienced internet sellers often overlook vintage electronics. This really is my specialty. I have made a good chunk of money <u>selling vintage electronics and parts</u>, especially audio equipment and vintage computers and accessories.

Why are these items so valuable? It is not just the resale of the whole units that make this niche so easy to make money on. Many collectors enjoy reconstructing these units or pimping out home-made systems with vintage components, which have unique properties that current electronics cannot mimic. Even broken electronics can be parted out for excellent money.

Not only that, but vintage electronics contain a significant amount of high profit scrap metal, like gold and silver in their contacts. My book 'Almost Free Money' has several chapters that readers have been raving about, and we also have a webpage devoted to teaching folks how to make money from Vintage Electronics.

7 *Used Power Tools and Hand Tools:*

If I were looking to specialize in only one niche, it may be in the used tools niche.

Used tools can be found in abundance at yard sales and estate sales, and people buy a LOT of used tools online, especially power tools. They are often modestly priced at garage sales, as well. You can make excellent profits selling used power tools, and not a lot of people realize that you can sell them on Amazon (where you can make more money than on eBay, without paying for listing fees).

You can also make a lot of money selling power tool accessories such as rechargeable batteries, chargers, and bits. There is an excellent opportunity in <u>reconditioning and reselling rechargeable batteries</u>, at profits of up to $50-60 each. You can find batteries for free in broken power tools, and often people will give them to you for free. What do you have to lose?!

6 *Used CDs and Music:*

I have made good money by selling used CDs that I found at garage sales. CDs are plentiful at garage sales, and they are quick and easy to sell on Amazon. A large box of CDs can be made available for sale on the Amazon marketplace in about twenty minutes. CDs are also easy to store and ship. They are also often found in <u>Free boxes</u> at yard sales.

However, CDs are quickly being phased out by the MP3 format. Many people are selling their CDs as they transfer over to MP3s, so prices have come down on the internet. Still, there is a robust market for CDs, especially in some niches.

5 *Gold, Silver and other Precious Metals:*

Yes, this stuff CAN be found at garage sales. I have found 24K gold jewelry mixed in with costume jewelry, sterling silver for $1, and I have even discovered gold and silver in free boxes!

Do your research so you can learn to ID precious metals, when they are mixed in with other items, and learn how to figure out value of gold items, in particular. At $1800 a troy ounce, you do not have to find much gold to make an excellent profit.

4 *Used Clothing:*

There is used clothing at almost every garage sale and yard sale that you will visit. Often, you can get quality used items for $1, or under. There are a lot of items that can be resold for consistent cash.

Garage sale investors can also find some excellent vintage collectible clothing at senior citizen's garage sales. I still think that this is going to be a goldmine very soon.

Not only do people collect vintage clothing like jeans, jackets, suits, shoes, and hats, vintage styles are also getting extremely popular among fashion-conscious jet-setters. This is especially true overseas.

Check out our Selling Used Clothing page for examples of what is hot now, and how to sell used clothing on eBay.

3 Vintage Collectibles:

Before the eBay explosion in the mid-1990s, vintage collectibles were the #1 niche, in terms of resale profits from garage sales and yard sales. In the 90s, it was common to find rare collectibles and resell them for high profit margins.

Now, an abundance of internet sellers and increased awareness by the general public about the value of many collectibles has driven the profit margins on collectibles down considerably. Still, there is good money to be made on a wide array of collectibles.

The most important tool a garage sale shopper has is their knowledge of collectibles. If you are interested in selling in this competitive selling niche, you HAVE to do your research. Know how to ID collectible items, and be familiar with what is selling well on eBay. Look at eBay Completed Listings and make notes, so that you know what to look for.

There are hundreds of niches for collectors, and there are many fun and interesting collectibles that you can resell on eBay.

The question is not "What is collectible?". It is "What is collectible and valuable?" If anybody ever thought something was cool, it is probably collected. It's just a matter of determining if the items will bring you enough profit to buy them at a garage sale.

2 *Video Games, Consoles, and Accessories*:

Selling used video games is probably the hottest internet selling niche right now. Experts predict that the video game market will double again over the next 10 years.

Finding used video games and consoles at garage sales is common. Gamers are constantly upgrading systems and discarding their beaten games.

Who sells these video games at garage sales? Yep... you guessed it... Moms and Grandmas. They do not know the value of vintage video games, which are sizzling hot among video game collectors now, especially Atari 2600, Nintendo NES, original Gameboy systems, and ColecoVision).

Even if consoles are often overpriced at garage sales, the games, controllers, and other accessories are often woefully underpriced. You can also "steal" consoles that are missing cords, or have minor repair issues.

Video games have the highest resale percentage of the Top 10 niches on this countdown, and are probably the fastest selling used items on Amazon.

Games, consoles, and accessories can all be listed quickly on Amazon. Video games take up very little storage area, and they are easy to ship.

Games can be found at many garage sales for $1, or under, and I have even found many video games in FREE boxes! Our Selling Used Video Games webpage is one of our hottest pages. It offers advice on how to sell video games, and some excellent links to careers in testing video games, and entering the video game business.

1 *Used Books*:

Used Books takes the top spot because of their versatility, availability, and potential for huge profits. You are more likely to find a big score with a rare book, collectible 1st edition, or signed book than you are with any other category of items in this countdown.

You can also use your smartphone and a price check application, so that you know exactly what you can make on books, before you even buy them.

Profitable books are readily available at most garage sales and yard sales, and you WILL find $50-100 books regularly, once you start buying them.

Books are easy to store on bookshelves, and listing books on Amazon and packaging and shipping books is a very efficient process.